"This generation of Christians inhabit cultures that sometimes reject not only biblical revelation about reality, but also the reality of reality itself. The Questions for Restless Minds series poses many of the toughest questions faced by young Christians to some of the world's foremost Christian thinkers and leaders. Along the way, this series seeks to help the Christian next generation to learn how to think biblically when they face questions in years to come that perhaps no one yet sees coming."

—Russell Moore,

public theologian, *Christianity Today*

"If you're hungry to go deeper in your faith, wrestle with hard questions, and are dissatisfied with the shallow content on your social media newsfeed, you'll really appreciate this series of thoughtful deep dives on critically important topics like faith, the Bible, friendship, sexuality, philosophy, and more. As you engage with some world-class Christian scholars, you'll be encouraged, equipped, challenged, and above all invited to love God more with your heart, soul, mind, and strength."

—Andy Kim,

multiethnic resource director, InterVarsity Christian Fellowship

T0385449

"In *Are All Religions True?*, Harold Netland tackles a difficult—yet important—question: 'How should Christians think theologically about the diverse variety of religious expression in light of God's revelation in Jesus Christ?' Having reflected thoughtfully on these issues for many years, Netland offers readers a helpful theological roadmap to navigate the complex terrain of Christian conversation on religious diversity. He shows how one can be faithful to Christ's universal lordship while treating adherents of non-Christian religions with dignity and honor."

—Keith E. Johnson,
author of *Rethinking the Trinity and Religious Pluralism*;
director of theological development and culture, Cru

Are All Religions True?

Questions for Restless Minds

Questions for Restless Minds

QUESTIONS FOR RESTLESS MINDS

Are All Religions True?

Harold A. Netland

D. A. Carson,
Series Editor

LEXHAM PRESS

Are All Religions True?
Questions for Restless Minds, edited by D. A. Carson

Copyright 2022 Christ on Campus Initiative

Lexham Press, 1313 Commercial St., Bellingham, WA 98225
LexhamPress.com

Print ISBN 9781683595014
Digital ISBN 9781683595021
Library of Congress Control Number 2021937691

Lexham Editorial: Todd Hains, Abigail Stocker, Mandi Newell
Cover Design: Brittany Schrock
Typesetting: Abigail Stocker

24 x / US

The Christ on Campus Initiative exists to inspire students on college and university campuses to think wisely, act with conviction, and become more Christlike by providing relevant and excellent evangelical resources on contemporary issues.

Visit christoncampuscci.org.

Contents

Series Preface

D. A. CARSON, SERIES EDITOR

T HE ORIGIN OF this series of books lies with a group of faculty from Trinity Evangelical Divinity School (TEDS), under the leadership of Scott Manetsch. We wanted to address topics faced by today's undergraduates, especially those from Christian homes and churches.

If you are one such student, you already know what we have in mind. You know that most churches, however encouraging they may be, are not equipped to prepare you for what you will face when you enroll at university.

It's not as if you've never known any winsome atheists before going to college; it's not as if you've never thought about Islam, or the credibility of the New Testament documents, or the nature of friendship, or gender identity, or how the claims of Jesus sound too exclusive and rather narrow, or the nature of evil. But up until now you've probably thought about such things within the shielding cocoon of a community of faith.

Now you are at college, and the communities in which you are embedded often find Christian perspectives to be at best oddly quaint and old-fashioned, if not repulsive. To use the current jargon, it's easy to become socialized into a new community, a new world.

How shall you respond? You could, of course, withdraw a little: just buckle down and study computer science or Roman history (or whatever your subject is) and refuse to engage with others. Or you could throw over your Christian heritage as something that belongs to your immature years and buy into the cultural package that surrounds you. Or—and this is what we hope you will do—you could become better informed.

But how shall you go about this? On any disputed topic, you do not have the time, and probably not the interest, to bury yourself in a couple of dozen volumes written by experts for experts. And if you did, that would be on *one* topic—and there are scores of topics that will grab the attention of the inquisitive student. On the other hand, brief pamphlets with predictable answers couched in safe slogans will prove to be neither attractive nor convincing.

So we have adopted a middle course. We have written short books pitched at undergraduates who want arguments that are accessible and stimulating, but invariably courteous. The material is comprehensive enough that it has become an important resource for pastors and other campus leaders who devote their energies to work with students. Each book ends with a brief annotated bibliography and study questions, intended for readers who want to probe a little further.

Lexham Press is making this series available as attractive print books and in digital formats (ebook and Logos resource). We hope and pray you will find them helpful and convincing.

INTRODUCTION

*N*ATHAN THE *WISE*, the last play written by the eighteenth-century philosopher and dramatist Gotthold Ephraim Lessing, contains a fascinating reworking of the classic parable of the three rings. The parable first appears in the fourteenth century in Boccaccio's *Decameron*, but Lessing modifies it slightly so that it expresses nicely the Enlightenment call for religious toleration and condemnation of religious dogmatism.[1] If it were updated slightly, it could be taken as an expression of early twenty-first-century views as well.

Lessing's version of the story is set in Jerusalem in the twelfth century during the Third Crusade. The play revolves around the complex relationships of three characters, each representative of one of the three great monotheistic religions: Nathan, a Jew; Saladin, a Muslim sultan; and a Christian Templar knight.

Nathan finds himself in the great Saladin's palace. The sultan tests Nathan by asking him which of the three monotheistic religions is the best. "You are so wise," he says to Nathan, "Now tell me, I entreat, what human faith, what theological law hath struck you as the truest and the best?"[2] Nathan prudently avoids a direct response and instead tells the parable of the three rings.

3

There was a man, says Nathan, who had an opal ring of supreme beauty and unusual powers. Whoever wore the ring was beloved by God and man. This ring had been passed down from generation to generation and now was the possession of this man who had three sons, each of whom he loved equally. At one time or another, the man had promised the ring to each of his sons. Sensing that he was about to die and realizing that he could not give the one ring to each of the three sons, the man secretly asked a master jeweller to make two perfect copies of the ring. The jeweller did such a good job that the man himself could not tell which was the original. At his deathbed, the man called each of his sons and gave him a ring and a blessing. After the father's death, the sons discovered that each one had a ring, and they began to argue among themselves as to which one possessed the original ring.

Commenting on their bickering, Nathan links their inability to identify the original ring to our inability to judge which is the one true religion:

> [The brothers] investigate, recriminate, and wrangle—
>   all in vain—
> Which was the true original genuine ring
> Was undemonstrable—
> Almost as much as now by us is undemonstrable
> The one true faith.[3]

The brothers then approach a wise judge to settle the dispute, but the judge responds by saying,

> If each of you in truth received his ring
> Straight from his father's hand, let each believe
> His own to be the true and genuine ring.[4]

After admonishing the brothers to quit trying to determine which is the original, the judge exhorts each son to accept his ring as if it were the true one and live a life of moral goodness, thereby bringing honor both to their father and to God.

Lessing's parable of the rings is an eloquent expression of eighteenth-century Enlightenment sentiment about monotheistic religion. Organized religion—especially the institutional Christian church—was dismissed as corrupt and blamed for the bloody wars of the previous century. Deep skepticism greeted claims of any particular religion being the one true faith. Weariness with religious in-fighting resulted in a kind of tolerance that regarded religions as worthy of acceptance only as long as they promote goodness and virtue and avoid dogmatism, which fuels religious strife.

Lessing's parable sounds remarkably contemporary. Today, as then, there is widespread skepticism about claims to exclusive truth in religion. Religions are assessed pragmatically on their capacity to produce morally respectable people. But there are also differences between Lessing's day and our own. We are today much more aware of the enormous religious diversity in our world, so that if we were to update the parable, we would need several dozen rings to symbolize the many available religious options, both monotheistic and nontheistic. In place of Saladin, we would have the beaming face of the Dalai Lama!

2

RELIGIOUS DIVERSITY AND CHRISTIAN FAITH

D<small>ESPITE THE PREDICTIONS</small> of some in the nineteenth century that religion would eventually wither away under the onslaught of modernization and science, the world today remains vigorously religious. Eighty percent of people worldwide profess some religious affiliation.[5] There are today roughly 2.1 billion Christians, 1.3 billion Muslims, 860 million Hindus, 380 million Buddhists, 25 million Sikhs, and 15 million Jews.[6] A complete picture of religion today would also include the many millions who follow one of the thousands of new religious movements.[7]

TRADITIONAL CHRISTIANITY: RELIGIOUS EXCLUSIVISM

Until the modern era, Christians largely took it for granted that Christianity is the one true religion for all humankind. Allowing for minor modifications for Orthodox, Roman Catholic, and Protestant distinctives, the common understanding went something like this: God has revealed himself in a special manner to the Old Testament patriarchs and prophets, and his self-revelation culminates in the incarnation of Jesus Christ (Heb 1:1–4). The written Scriptures—the Old and New Testaments—are the divinely inspired written revelation of God and thus are unlike any other sacred writings. Salvation is a gift of God's grace and is possible only because of the unique person and work of Jesus Christ on the cross. Sinful human beings are saved by God's grace through repentance of sin and faith. Thus, Jesus Christ is the one Savior and Lord for all people at all times.

On this view there is an inescapable particularity concerning Jesus Christ. While God's love and mercy are extended to all, salvation is limited to those who repent and accept by faith God's provision in Jesus Christ. Numerous biblical texts could be cited in support of this particularity: Peter declares, "There is salvation in no one else, for there is no other name under heaven given among men by which we must be saved" (Acts 4:12); Jesus responds to a question from Thomas by stating, "I am the way, and the truth, and the life. No one comes to the Father except through me" (John 14:6); the apostle Paul claims, "There is one God, and one mediator between God and men, the man Christ Jesus" (1 Tim 2:5); and so on.

The particularity of the Christian gospel has always been a stumbling block to many. It was widely accepted in the ancient Mediterranean world that the same deity could take on various forms and be called by different names in different cultures. According to historian Robert Wilken, "The oldest and most enduring criticism of Christianity is an appeal to religious pluralism. ... All the ancient critics of Christianity were united in affirming that there is no one way to the divine."[8] Significantly, it was within this context of religious syncretism and relativism that we find the New

Testament putting forward Jesus Christ as the one Savior for all people.

After the seventeenth century, the broad consensus among Christians concerning Christianity as the one true religion began to fragment, although it was not until the twentieth century that the full effects of this became evident. Many factors were involved in the erosion of confidence in traditional Christianity: widespread disillusionment at the rampant corruption of the institutional church; ongoing fighting among various "Christian" factions; the growing awareness of other peoples, cultures, and religions as a result of the European voyages of "discovery"; increased skepticism about our ability to know religious truth; and the effects of higher critical views of Scripture that treated the Bible as just one among many sacred texts. While Jesus was still revered as a great moral teacher, many openly questioned orthodox teachings about his deity, and suggested that Jesus was just one of many great religious figures through whom we might relate to God.

By the mid-twentieth century, the subject of the relation of Christian faith to other religions was a central concern of Christian theologians and missiologists with a surprising variety of perspectives.[9] Many, to be sure, remained firmly committed to the orthodox position. However, more liberal Protestants and post-Vatican II Roman Catholics adopted far more accommodating views of other religions and modified their views of Jesus Christ and salvation.

RELIGIOUS INCLUSIVISM

"Inclusivist" theologians, as they were often called, tried to keep in balance two divergent themes: (1) God's salvation is somehow based upon the person and work of Jesus Christ, and in this sense Jesus has a special relationship with God and is unlike any other religious figure; and (2) God's salvation made available in Christ is also available to adherents of other religions just as they are, so there is no need for followers of other religions to be converted to Christ. Thus, while the fullest expression of God's truth and revelation are in Jesus Christ and the Christian Scriptures, other religions can be accepted positively as part of God's plan for humankind.

RELIGIOUS PLURALISM

By the late twentieth century, however, there were growing numbers of those identifying themselves as Christians who explicitly rejected such inclusivistic views and called for a radical pluralism in which Christianity is just one among many possible ways of responding to the divine. Religious pluralism, as understood by these thinkers, means that all the major religions are more or less equally true and effective ways of responding to the religious ultimate; no single religion—including Christianity—can claim legitimately to be superior to others in terms of truth or in relating appropriately to the divine.

There are many reasons that religious pluralism, as defined above, is so attractive today. We are much more aware of religious diversity today, due to globalization, increased immigration, international travel, and the impact of media and the worldwide web. As the West encounters religious others, there is often the realization that Hindus, Buddhists, and Sikhs are not at all as previously imagined; they are often intelligent and morally respectable people who are similar to Westerners in many respects. Furthermore, in light of the tragic history of Western colonialism during the past four centuries, many have a deep sense of "post-colonialist guilt" over past injustices. It is often assumed that the way to atone for the past sins of colonialism is to accept uncritically other cultural and religious perspectives. The desire to affirm the increasing diversity of the West is often accompanied by the assumption that doing so means not rejecting other religions as false or somehow deficient. It is not surprising, then, that religious diversity is causing many, including Christians, to question traditional Christian perspectives. Peter Berger captures the spirit of the times when he observes,

> We do have a problem of belief, and it not only raises the question of why we should believe in God but why we should believe in *this* God. There are others, after all, and today they are made available in an unprecedented way through the religious supermarket of modern pluralism.[10]

Pluralistic perspectives are found today not just among academics; they are widely adopted in popular culture as well. Based upon an extensive study of American views on religious diversity, sociologist Robert Wuthnow reports that 42 percent of all respondents agreed with the statement, "All religions basically teach the same thing," and 46 percent said that they believed that God's word is revealed in other writings apart from the Bible, such as the sacred texts of Muslims or Hindus.[11]

3

CLARIFYING
THE ISSUES

W HEN IT COMES to the subject of Christian faith and other religions, we are dealing not with just one question but rather with a set of interrelated issues. Thus, it is important that we clarify issues and make some basic distinctions. A helpful place to begin is by considering the term "religious pluralism," for it is used in different ways.

RELIGIOUS DIVERSITY EXISTS

"Religious pluralism" can be used in a strictly descriptive sense to mean religious diversity. To say, then, that Europe or North America is religiously pluralistic means simply that they are increasingly characterized by religious diversity. This is undeniable, and by itself is not particularly controversial.

RELIGIOUS DIVERSITY SHOULD BE LEGALLY ACCEPTED

But more often "religious pluralism" includes more than merely the fact of religious diversity. The term usually connotes more or less positive attitudes toward such diversity, or acceptance, in some sense, of religious diversity. But there are varying degrees of acceptance. At a minimal level there is the *legal acceptance* of diversity. In many democratic societies today, there is an explicit legal commitment to freedom of religion. Sometimes, as in the United States, this is combined with the formal prohibition of governmental sanction of any particular religion. Most Christians welcome such guarantees of freedom of religion and acknowledge readily that such rights also apply to adherents of non-Christian religions.

RELIGIOUS DIVERSITY SHOULD BE SOCIALLY ACCEPTED

But the legal acceptance of religious diversity is, at best, a minimalist kind of acceptance. One can, for example, acknowledge the legal rights of, say, Hindus or Muslims to live in the United States but fail to grant them social acceptance as full members of American society. This suggests the importance of what we might call the *social acceptance* of religious others.

In a weaker sense, social acceptance might involve developing friendships with religious others and cooperating with them in a variety of social activities. But in this sense, social acceptance can be somewhat ambivalent, for while it accepts social relationships with religious others, it might also disapprove of, to some extent, what religious others represent. There is also a sense in which one does not approve of other religions.

A stronger sense of social acceptance includes an enthusiastic embrace of religious diversity as something good. Acceptance here goes well beyond mere tolerance to a celebration of religious diversity as something inherently positive. While the enthusiastic affirmation of religious diversity can be compatible with orthodox Christianity and the view that the Christian faith is distinctively true, it is often found among those who have reinterpreted traditional Christian teachings in various ways. Many in this category regard other religions, along with Christianity, as instruments through which God's truth and saving grace are mediated.

ALL MAJOR RELIGIONS ARE EQUALLY TRUE AND LEGITIMATE

As a technical term in religious studies and theology, however, "religious pluralism" refers to a view that goes well beyond just the social acceptance of religious others. *Religious pluralism* in this sense is the view that all of the major religions are (roughly) equally true and provide equally legitimate ways in which to respond to the divine reality. No single religion—including Christianity—can legitimately claim to be uniquely true and normative for all people in all cultures at all times. It is in this sense that we will be using the term "religious pluralism" throughout this book.

4

JOHN HICK'S MODEL OF RELIGIOUS PLURALISM

P ETER BYRNE, a contemporary advocate of religious pluralism, states three propositions that are at the heart of religious pluralism:

> Pluralism as a theoretical response to religious diversity can now be summarily defined by three propositions. (1) All major forms of religion are equal in respect of making common reference to a single, transcendent sacred reality. (2) All major forms of religion are likewise equal in respect of offering some means or other to human salvation. (3) All religious traditions are to be seen as containing revisable, limited accounts of the nature of the sacred: none is certain enough in its particular dogmatic formulations to provide the norm for interpreting the others.[12]

These points are foundational to the perspective of religious pluralism advanced by theologian and philosopher John Hick, perhaps the most influential religious pluralist today. Hick began his academic career in the 1950s as an able defender of Christian orthodoxy, but by the early 1980s, he had abandoned Christian theism for a thoroughgoing religious pluralism.[13] Three claims are at the center of his model of religious pluralism: (1) there is a religious ultimate reality—what Hick calls "the Real"—to which the major religions are all legitimate responses; (2) the various religions are historically and culturally conditioned interpretations of this divine reality; and (3) salvation/enlightenment/liberation is to be understood as the moral transformation of people from self-centeredness to Reality-centeredness, and it is occurring roughly to the same extent across the major religions. Accordingly, Hick claims that the religions can be regarded as culturally and historically conditioned human responses to

> an ultimate ineffable Reality which is the source and ground of everything, and which is such that in so far as the religious traditions are in soteriological alignment with it they are contexts of salvation/liberation. These traditions involve different human conceptions of the Real, with correspondingly different forms of experience of the Real, and correspondingly different forms of life in response to the Real.[14]

The various religions, then, are to be accepted as, in principle, equally legitimate religious alternatives with choices among them being largely functions of individual preferences and socio-cultural influences. The religions "constitute different human responses to the ultimate transcendent reality to which they all, in their different ways, bear witness."[15]

But if the religions all are responding to the same divine reality, why is there such bewildering diversity in the ways in which people understand this reality? Why is there not greater agreement among the religions? Hick accounts for diversity in belief and practice by appealing to historical and cultural factors: "We always perceive the transcendent through the lens of a particular religious culture with its distinctive set of concepts, myths, historical exemplars and devotional or meditational techniques."[16] Although ultimately it is the same divine reality that is encountered in the religions, both the awareness of and response to this reality are shaped by contingent historical and cultural factors.

Now Hick is well aware of the fact that the religions do not all agree on the nature of the religious ultimate. Some religions regard the religious ultimate in personal categories, such as Yahweh in Judaism, or God the Holy Trinity in Christianity, or Allah in Islam, or as Shiva or Krishna in theistic forms of Hinduism. Other religions depict the religious ultimate in nonpersonal categories, such as Nirguna Brahman in Advaita Vedanta Hinduism, or Sunyata or Emptiness in Buddhism, or the Dao in Daoism. Hick refers to the former as the divine *personae* and the latter as the divine *impersonae*. He maintains that what is truly religiously ultimate—the Real—transcends both the *personae* and *impersonae* and thus cannot be characterized as either personal or nonpersonal. So the Real cannot be identified with Yahweh or the Holy Trinity or Sunyata or the Dao. These are merely penultimate symbols through which people in various religions understand and respond to what is actually ultimate, the Real. Out of a desire not to privilege either personal or nonpersonal ways of thinking about the religious ultimate, Hick insists that none of the characteristics of the *personae* or the *impersonae* can be attributed to the Real.

> The distinction between the Real as it is in itself and as it is thought and experienced through our human religious concepts entails … that we cannot apply to the Real *an sich* [as it is in itself] the characteristics encountered in its *personae* and *impersonae*. Thus, it cannot be said to be one or many, person or thing, conscious or unconscious, purposive or non-purposive, substance or process, good or evil, loving or hating. None of the descriptive terms that apply within the realm of human experience can apply literally to the unexperienced reality that underlies that realm.[17]

Hick thus accepts a strong version of what is called the ineffability thesis, so that none of the terms and concepts that we ordinarily use in religious discourse can be applied to the Real.

Given the clear differences in conceptions of the religious ultimate in the religions, why should we postulate the Real as the common ground of the religions? Hick explains:

> My reason to assume that the different world religions are referring, through their specific concepts

of the Gods and Absolutes, to the same ultimate Reality is the striking similarity of the transformed human state described within the different traditions as saved, redeemed, enlightened, wise, awakened, liberated. This similarity strongly suggests a common source of salvific transformation.[18]

Understood as "the transformation from self-centeredness to Reality-centeredness," salvation, according to Hick, is said to be evident in roughly the same degree in all the religions.

It may be that one [religion] facilitates human liberation/salvation more than the others, but if so this is not evident to human vision. So far as we can tell, they are equally productive of that transition from self to Reality which we see in the saints of all traditions.[19]

Although a pluralist, Hick still identifies himself as a Christian, and thus he includes a place for Jesus in his model. Hick, however, clearly rejects the traditional, orthodox view of Jesus as fully God and fully man, the unique incarnation of God. Rather, he adopts a metaphorical interpretation of the incarnation and Jesus' relation to God.

[Jesus] was so powerfully God conscious that his life vibrated, as it were, to the divine life; and as a result his hands could heal the sick, and the "poor in spirit" were kindled to new life in his presence. … Thus in Jesus' presence, we should have felt that we are in the presence of God—not in the sense that the man Jesus literally *is* God, but in the sense that he was so totally conscious of God that we could catch something of that consciousness by spiritual contagion.[20]

For Hick, then, the incarnation "is a mythological idea, a figure of speech, a piece of poetic imagery. It is a way of saying that Jesus is our living contact with the transcendent God. In his presence we find that we are brought into the presence of God."[21] On this view, could we not think in terms of multiple incarnations? Responding affirmatively, Hick says that "it becomes entirely natural to say that all the great religious figures have in their different ways 'incarnated' the ideal of human life in response to the one divine Reality."[22]

Hick's proposal is obviously a very different view of Jesus Christ and other religions than what the Church has affirmed throughout the centuries. But it is easy to see the enormous attraction that religious pluralism has for many today. For with Hick's pluralism, all the major religions can be embraced as more or less equally true and effective ways of relating to the divine. Religious disputes can be avoided, and there is no need for evangelism or conversion; Christians can simply cooperate with those from other religions in alleviating the many problems confronting humankind.

But the crucial issue here is not whether religious pluralism is attractive, but whether it is the best way to think about the relation among the religions. Despite its many attractive qualities, religious pluralism faces formidable problems. Before exploring the difficulties with pluralism, however, it will be helpful to consider further the concept of religion and religious beliefs.

5

RELIGIONS AND RELIGIOUS BELIEFS

ALTHOUGH DISCUSSIONS OF religious pluralism typically focus upon the "great religions"—by which is usually meant Judaism, Christianity, Islam, Hinduism, and Buddhism—it is important to remember also the many other religious traditions that make up the religious mosaic of the world, both past and present. There are, for example, the religions of the ancient world, of the ancient Egyptians and Babylonians, the Greeks and Romans, and the Aztecs and Incas. We must also include the many new religious movements of the modern world, some of which—such as Baha'i and Mormonism—have developed into world religions in their own right. There are also the many less clearly defined religious movements, such as "new age" spirituality, as well as modernized versions of ancient traditions, including Celtic Druidry or Maori religion.

While it is easy enough to identify examples of religions (Islam, Christianity, Hinduism, etc.), it is much more difficult to come up with an acceptable definition of religion. Definitions tend to be either too broad, thus applying to things that we do not normally include as religious, or too narrow, excluding things that we do regard as religious. The difficulty here stems from the great diversity we find among religious traditions. Nevertheless, the following definition by Roger Schmidt and his colleagues is adequate for most purposes: "Religions are systems of meaning embodied in a pattern of life, a community of faith, and a worldview that articulate a view of the sacred and of what ultimately matters."[23]

Religions are multifaceted phenomena and there is some overlap between the concepts of religion and culture. This is made clear in the very helpful suggestion by Ninian Smart that we think in terms of seven dimensions of religion.[24] These include the ritual, narrative, experiential, doctrinal, ethical, social, and material dimensions of religion. If we are to understand a particular religion such as Buddhism or Christianity, we must give due attention to all seven dimensions.

Religions, then, include much more than just beliefs or doctrines. Nevertheless, beliefs are central to religion. A religious community is expected to live in a certain way and to regard all of life from a particular perspective. A particular religious tradition can be thought of as expressing a distinctive worldview, or way of understanding reality, and adherents of that tradition are expected to embrace that worldview.

At the heart of each religious worldview are some basic beliefs about the nature of the cosmos, the religious ultimate, and the relation of humankind to this ultimate. Religious beliefs are significant, for as Smart observes, "The world religions owe some of their living power to their success in presenting a total picture of reality, through a coherent system of doctrines."[25] Religious believers are expected to accept the teachings of their tradition and to pattern their lives in accordance with such beliefs. The worldviews of the various religions can be clarified by posing three basic questions to the religions: (1) What is the nature of the religious ultimate? (2) What is the nature of the human predicament? (3) What is the nature of and conditions for attaining salvation/liberation/enlightenment? We will consider briefly how Hinduism, Buddhism, and Islam address these questions.

WHAT IS THE NATURE OF
THE RELIGIOUS ULTIMATE?

Hinduism is a family of many different traditions that are the product of some 4,000 years of development in India. Hinduism includes a variety of views about the religious ultimate. A Hindu may believe in one God, many gods, or no god. The idea that the religious ultimate can be understood and experienced in many different ways is widely accepted. Most Hindus, however, accept Brahman as the Supreme Being and sustaining power of the cosmos. But there is disagreement over the nature of Brahman and its relation to the human person. Hinduism includes both monistic and theistic traditions. The Advaita Vedanta (Non-Dualism) tradition, for example, claims that the sole reality is Nirguna Brahman, a nonpersonal reality utterly beyond human concepts and categories. The Vishisht Advaita (Qualified Non-Dualism) teaches that there is only one reality, Saguna Brahman, or Brahman with personal

Chapter 5 | Religions and Religious Beliefs

attributes. Brahman is thus a personal Being, and the world is the "body" of Brahman.

Buddhism originated from the teachings of Siddhartha Gautama (traditionally, 563–483 BC), who was determined to find the cause of suffering and pain. After much meditation and ascetic discipline, Gautama experienced an "awakening" or "enlightenment," and for the next forty years he traveled throughout India preaching the *dharma* (truth) and attracting a large following. A variety of terms are used for the religious ultimate in Buddhism. For the Theravada tradition it is *nirvana*, which alone is permanent, unconditioned, and ultimately real. But *nirvana* is not heaven; it is the state that a person obtains when the fires of desire and the conditions producing rebirth are eliminated. The ultimate reality in Mahayana Buddhism is the *Dharmakaya*, or the all-inclusive Buddha essence, sometimes called the Void or Emptiness (*Sunyata*). Neither *nirvana* nor the *Dharmakaya* can be thought of as a personal being. Buddhism clearly rejects any idea of an all-powerful creator God; in this sense it is atheistic.

Islam maintains that Muhammad (ca. AD 570–632) was the last and greatest in a long line of prophets sent from God. Muhammad received revelations from Allah that are contained in the Qur'an, which is understood by Muslims to be the word of God. All branches of Islam embrace a strict monotheism. The religious ultimate is Allah, the one God, creator of everything else that exists. Islam calls for total submission to Allah's sovereign will in all of life.

WHAT IS THE NATURE OF THE HUMAN PREDICAMENT?

According to classical Hinduism, the human predicament consists in the repeated reincarnation of the *atman* (the soul) as it passes from one life to another. Repeated births are regulated by *karma*, a metaphysical principle that determines current and future states on the basis of past actions and dispositions. The traditional soteriological goal of Hinduism is *moksha*, or liberation from rebirths through breaking the causal conditions of *karma*.

The human predicament in Buddhism consists in our being trapped in a cycle of repeated rebirths and the fact that all existence—apart from *nirvana*—is characterized by pervasive suffering or dissatisfaction. The goal in classical Buddhism, then, is to break the chain of causal conditions resulting in rebirths, thereby attaining *nirvana*. The Four Noble Truths present a diagnosis of the cause of suffering (desire or attachment) and a way to the elimination of suffering. The Noble Eightfold Path sets out ideals in moral self-discipline, meditation, and wisdom that provide the way to eliminate desire and thereby suffering.[26]

In Islam, the human predicament consists of the fact that human beings do not submit to Allah and his ways but rather disobey his will, thereby producing the evil and suffering in our world. Human beings have a weakness of will and a general tendency toward sin. But although tempted by Iblis (the Devil), it is within the power of humankind to resist evil and to remain faithful to the will of Allah.

WHAT IS THE NATURE OF
AND THE CONDITIONS FOR
ATTAINING SALVATION/
LIBERATION/ENLIGHTENMENT?

Traditionally in Hinduism there are three ways to attain liberation. (1) The way of right action (*karma marga*) involves living in accordance with one's duty as determined by gender, caste, and stage in life. (2) The way of liberating knowledge (*jnana marga*) is advocated by Advaita Vedanta, which teaches that what breaks the cycle of rebirths is the existential realization of one's own essential identity with Brahman. (3) The way of devotion (*bhakti marga*) involves love, reverence, or adoration for a particular deity, and performing ritual worship of deities such as Vishnu, Shiva, or Krishna.

Different schools of Buddhism have slightly different teachings, but most Theravada traditions emphasize strict adherence to the Noble Eightfold Path, which includes proper understanding of the nature of reality—including the Buddha's teaching on the impermanence of all things—and rigorous meditation. Mahayana traditions tend to emphasize seeking enlightenment in this life through meditation. Theravada Buddhism emphasizes self-effort in attaining *nirvana*; each person is said to be responsible for attaining his or her own liberation, which is restricted to the few who can master the required disciplines. Mahayana opened the way to the masses by acknowledging a vast multitude of spiritual beings, such as the *bodhisattvas*, who assist in the quest for enlightenment and liberation.

Islam teaches that our present world will one day be destroyed by Allah and that all humankind, past and present, will then be raised to face divine judgment. In the judgment each person's deeds will be impartially weighed in the balance. Salvation is strictly on the basis of submission to Allah and faithful adherence to the teachings of Islam. Some will be admitted to paradise; others consigned to hell. Islam denies the need for a savior and the substitutionary atonement, as found in Christianity.

6

THE
PROBLEM OF
CONFLICTING
TRUTH CLAIMS

As seen above, the major religions acknowledge that our world is not as it should be; there is a deeply rooted problem that needs to be addressed. The religions offer different perspectives on what the problem is and how it can be overcome. The Indian religions—such as Hinduism and Buddhism—typically adopt a medical analogy in expressing their views. Using this analogy, the philosopher Keith Yandell reminds us that the concept of truth is embedded in the deep structure of religious worldviews:

> A religion proposes a diagnosis of a deep, crippling spiritual disease universal to non-divine sentience and offers a cure. A particular religion is true if its diagnosis is correct and its cure efficacious. The diagnosis and cure occur in the setting of an account of what there is—an account whose truth is assumed by the content of the diagnosis and cure.[27]

In other words, the concept of truth is central to the religions. But how should we understand religious truth? In religion, as in other domains, truth is fundamentally a property of statements or propositions, and by extension, of beliefs. A statement or belief is true if and only if the state of affairs to which the statement refers is as the statements asserts. Otherwise it is false. Thus, the statement

"The universe was created by God" is true if and only if the universe was in fact created by God. The belief that "The only reality not undergoing continual change is *nirvana*" is true if and only if the only reality not undergoing continual change is *nirvana*. And so on. Religious beliefs, like other beliefs, can be clear or vague, easy to understand or difficult to interpret. (True statements in physics or history can also be vague or difficult to understand.) None of that affects their truth status.[28]

The fact of religious diversity leads to the problem of conflicting truth claims. Diversity by itself, of course, does not necessarily indicate disagreement. Moreover, we should acknowledge that there are some commonalities among the religions (e.g., the ethical principle behind the Golden Rule is reflected in the teachings of many religions). Nevertheless, it is clear that Buddhists, Christians, Hindus, and Muslims adopt fundamentally different perspectives on basic questions about the religious ultimate and our relation to this reality. Christians and Muslims, for example, believe that the universe was created by an eternal Creator; Buddhists deny this. Advaita Vedanta Hindus maintain that the ultimate reality is Nirguna Brahman; Buddhists reject this. Christians insist that Jesus Christ was the incarnate Word of God, fully God and fully man; Muslims dismiss this as blasphemous.

While all of the religions acknowledge that the present state of the world is not as it should be, they disagree over the cause of this unsatisfactory state and its proper remedy.

For Christians, the root cause is sin against a holy God and the cure consists in repentance and reconciliation with God through the atoning work of Jesus Christ on the cross. For Buddhists and Hindus the cause lies in a pervasive ignorance, a fundamentally mistaken view of reality—although they disagree sharply among themselves over just which beliefs are false and should be rejected. Hindus believe in enduring, substantial souls which are reincarnated in multiple lives. Buddhists deny that there is an enduring, substantial soul which passes from one life to another.

In this respect, differences among the religions take the form of basic disagreements over the nature of reality, how we have arrived at the current undesirable state of affairs, and how we can attain a more desirable state. Disagreements between Christianity and Theravada Buddhism, for example, over how to attain the desired goal—whether one should repent of one's sins and accept Jesus Christ as Lord and Savior or follow the Noble Eightfold Path—are not disputes over the proper means to a common goal but rather grow out of radically different understandings of reality and thus different ends that are to be pursued. While there certainly are points of agreement among the religions, it is clear that at least some of the claims by the major religions are mutually incompatible. They might all be wrong, but they cannot all be correct.

It is sometimes said that this way of thinking about religious beliefs—that religious beliefs, like other propositions, are true or false, and that two contradictory beliefs cannot both be true—is merely a Western way of understanding religion and that Eastern religions do not approach religion in this manner. Rational approaches to religion that emphasize logical consistency depend upon "Western logic," and other religions are not necessarily limited by such logical constraints. Therefore, it is said, the problem of conflicting truth claims is really a pseudo-problem, since it relies upon logical assumptions that not all religions share.

Although this perspective is fairly common, it is inadequate and very misleading. First, there is the empirical or factual question whether Western thought emphasizes rationality and logical consistency and whether Eastern thought rejects rational approaches to religion. What exactly is "Western" or "Eastern" thought? These are not monolithic entities but rather are broad abstractions that refer to large collections of people who display enormous diversity in thought. It is true that many people in Europe and North America do emphasize the importance of reason and logical consistency, but many others do not. Particularly in religious practice and the academic study of religion, many in the West today reject rational and logical principles, maintaining that religious "truth" somehow transcends rational categories. Similarly, there are religious traditions in Asia, such as certain forms of Hinduism, Buddhism (especially Zen), and Daoism, which do reject dependence on rational principles in the pursuit of religious "truth." But many other religious traditions, especially in India and to some extent in China, are highly rational and emphasize the importance of logical consistency in belief.

Consider, for example, the comments of the Sri Lankan Buddhist scholar K. N. Jayatilleke. After arguing that the Buddha actually embraced the correspondence theory of truth, he asserts that for Buddhists inconsistency is a criterion of falsehood:

> Although correspondence with fact is considered to be the essential characteristic of truth, consistency or coherence is also held to be a criterion. In contrast, inconsistency is a criterion of falsehood. In arguing with his opponents, the Buddha often shows that their theories lead to inconsistencies or contradictions, thereby demonstrating that they are false, using what is known as the Socratic method. ... This means that truth must be consistent. Therefore, when a number of theories with regard to the nature of man and his destiny in the universe contradict each other, they cannot all be true, though they could all be false if none of them correspond with fact.[29]

Similarly, the Japanese Buddhist scholar Hajime Nakamura claims,

> Gotama was described as one who reasoned according to the truth rather than on the basis of the authority of the Vedas or tradition. Theravada

and Mahayana Buddhism have accepted two stan-
dards for the truth of a statement: it must be in
accord with the [Buddhist] scriptures and must be
proved true by reasoning. No Buddhist is expected
to believe anything which does not meet these two
tests.[30]

Thus, it simply is not the case that "Eastern thought" in
general rejects rational principles such as the principle of
noncontradiction.

But even if a particular tradition—perhaps Zen
Buddhism or Daoism—does reject the principle of noncontradiction, it does not follow that such rational principles are merely Western and do not apply in other contexts.
There is an important distinction between rejecting a belief
or principle and refuting it. All kinds of beliefs have been
rejected by people at one time or another. The issue is not
whether a belief is rejected but whether it *should* be rejected.
To refute a belief or principle is to show that it is false or at
least that there are compelling reasons not to accept it as
true. Although many people—both in the West as well as
the East—reject the principle of noncontradiction in religion, no one has refuted the principle. It is impossible to
refute the principle, since any attempt at refutation necessarily appeals to the very principle one is trying to refute.[31]
Any meaningful assertion about anything at all—including
religious assertions—if intended to be true, makes implicit
appeal to the principle by ruling out its negation as false.

7

RELIGIOUS EXCLUSIVISM

The New Testament never suggests that Jesus is one among many possible saviors. The consistent witness of the Bible is that God has revealed himself in an utterly unique manner through the Scriptures and the incarnation and that Jesus Christ is the one Lord and Savior for all people. Such particularistic themes are often taken as evidence that Christianity is exclusive in ways that other religions—such as Hinduism or Buddhism—are not.

But it is important to recognize that other major religions, including the Indian religions, also have exclusivistic tendencies in that each regards its own perspective as distinctively true and thus superior to other alternatives. In both Buddhism and Hinduism, liberation is linked to a correct understanding of the nature of reality, and each religion rejects what it regards as false views on the grounds that they impede liberation. Buddhism, for example, claims to tell the truth about how things are, and other accounts that are incompatible with Buddhist teachings are dismissed as mistaken, resulting in ignorance and further suffering. For Buddhists, only Buddhism leads to release from the ignorance giving rise to suffering.

There have been vigorous debates among Hindus, Buddhists, and Jains (Jainism is another Indian religious system distinct from Hinduism and Buddhism) over rival religious claims.[32] Shankara (d. 820), who shaped Advaita Vedanta Hinduism, forthrightly states, "If the soul . . . is not considered to possess fundamental unity with Brahman— an identity to be realized by knowledge—there is not any chance of its obtaining final release."[33] In other words, only if one accepts the central teaching of Advaita Vedanta can one be liberated. Early Buddhists rejected Hindu assumptions about Brahman and the reality of enduring souls which reincarnate. Similarly, a text from the Jaina Sutras, the authoritative texts of Jainism, bluntly states,

> Those who do not know all things by Kevala [the absolute knowledge sought by Jains], but who being ignorant teach a Law [contrary to Jain teaching], are lost themselves, and work the ruin of others in this dreadful, boundless Circle of Births. Those who know all things by the full Kevala knowledge, and who practicing meditation teach the whole Law, are themselves saved and save others.[34]

In other words, those who accept Jain doctrine can be enlightened and liberated from rebirths; those who do not, cannot be enlightened.

Nor are these merely ancient perspectives. The Dalai Lama, for example, in responding to the question whether only the Buddha can provide "the ultimate source of refuge," says,

Here, you see, it is necessary to examine what is meant by liberation or salvation. Liberation in which "a mind that understands the sphere of reality annihilates all defilements in the sphere of reality" is a state that only Buddhists can accomplish. This kind of *moksha* [liberation] or *nirvana* is only explained in the Buddhist scriptures, and is achieved only through Buddhist practice.[35]

The theme in these passages is clear enough: beliefs matter, and proper acceptance of the relevant teachings is essential for attaining liberation. Those who hold certain false beliefs cannot achieve liberation or enlightenment. Hindus, Buddhists, and Jains, of course, disagree on just which beliefs are false.

8

PROBLEMS
WITH RELIGIOUS
PLURALISM

RELIGIOUS PLURALISM PROMISES a way of understanding religious diversity without concluding that only one religion is true and the rest false. All the major religions are said to be more or less equally true and equally legitimate ways of responding to the religious ultimate. Pluralism thus seems to be accepting the many religions just as they are, and in a world weary of religious competition and strife, this is indeed enormously attractive.

But can the pluralist model really deliver what it promises? An acceptable model of religious pluralism should do at least three things: (1) recognize the clear differences in fundamental beliefs among the religions; (2) affirm the different religions as more or less equally effective ways of responding to the one ultimate reality, so that no single tradition is privileged; and (3) provide a coherent explanation of how these two points can be simultaneously maintained. John Hick's proposal is the most sophisticated attempt to meet these requirements, but it is vitiated by serious problems. Two issues will be noted.

SOME TRUTH CLAIMS
CANNOT BOTH BE TRUE

Contrary to popular perception, not even the pluralist can avoid the conclusion that large numbers of sincere and devout religious believers are simply mistaken in their religious beliefs. As we have seen, if the teachings of the religions are taken as orthodox believers in the respective religions understand them, it is clear that the religions make very different, and at times mutually incompatible, claims about the nature of reality. Each religion of course maintains that its own beliefs are true. With religious pluralism, however, no particular religion can be regarded as distinctively true. Thus, the conflicting claims of the religions are reinterpreted so that they can be accommodated in a pluralist framework.

Consider beliefs about the religious ultimate that are central to Christianity, Islam, and Buddhism, respectively. Christians believe that the religious ultimate, the highest reality, is the Triune God—Father, Son, and Holy Spirit, and that Jesus Christ was the incarnate Son of God, fully God and fully man. Muslims also believe in one eternal creator God, but deny that God is a trinity or that Jesus was God incarnate. Zen Buddhists deny the existence of any God and maintain that ultimate reality is *Sunyata* or Emptiness. On Hick's model, Christians, Muslims, and Buddhists can all be said to be "in touch" with and responding appropriately to the one divine reality, the Real. So in one sense John Hick's pluralism does accept the three religions, but it does so only by changing in important ways the beliefs of actual Christians, Muslims, and Buddhists. For on Hick's model, it is the Real that is truly ultimate, and what Christians, Muslims, and Buddhists regard as ultimate—the Triune God, Allah, and Emptiness, respectively—are only penultimate images or concepts through which they respond to the Real. If Hick is correct, then orthodox Christians, Muslims, and Buddhists are all mistaken in their claims about the religious ultimate.

Or consider what Islam and Christianity say about Jesus of Nazareth. Although Jesus is held in great esteem in both Christianity and Islam, the two religions disagree sharply over his proper identity. Christians accept Jesus as the unique incarnation of the eternal, infinite, God—Jesus was fully God and fully man. Muslims, on the other hand, reject this as blasphemous. Furthermore, Christians and Muslims disagree over the factual question whether Jesus was in fact crucified on the cross, for many Muslims interpret Surah 4:155–159 of the Qur'an as explicitly ruling out Jesus' death on the cross. This cannot be dismissed as merely a minor disagreement over an obscure historical fact, for the atoning work of Jesus on the cross is central to the Christian message of salvation. Thus it has traditionally been maintained that Islam and Christianity cannot both be correct in their respective beliefs about Jesus of Nazareth. At least one view must be false. As we have seen, John Hick rejects the orthodox Christian teaching of Jesus as fully God and fully man and calls for a reinterpretation of the doctrine of the incarnation in metaphorical terms. The implication of this, however, is that orthodox Christians are mistaken in their belief about the incarnation. Thus, not even religious pluralism can avoid the conclusion that large numbers of sincere and intelligent religious believers are mistaken in their religious beliefs. The critical issue here is which beliefs we should reject as false and on what basis we should do so.

INEFFABILITY IS INCOHERENT

Not surprisingly, Hick's adoption of strong ineffability with respect to the Real has been the subject of much criticism. In order not to privilege either personal or non-personal views of the religious ultimate, Hick insists that the Real transcends all concepts and properties with which we are familiar.

> By "ineffable" I mean … having a nature that is beyond the scope of our networks of human concepts. Thus the Real in itself cannot properly be said to be personal or impersonal, purposive or non-purposive, good or evil, substance or process, even one or many.[36]

There are at least three problems with Hick's use of the ineffability thesis:

1. Although Hick claims that none of the concepts or categories with which we are familiar can be applied to the Real, he repeatedly uses language that presupposes that at least *some* concepts do apply meaningfully to the Real.[37] For the Real is said to be the "source and ground of everything," a "transcendent reality," "the necessary condition of our existence

and highest good," "that to which religion is a response," to "affect humanity," to have a "universal presence," etc.[38] If such language is at all meaningful, then clearly some concepts can be applied to the Real. Moreover, it seems that causality of some sort is implied in such language, as the Real is portrayed as (at least partially) causally responsible for the human religious responses being what they are. But in using the language of causality in this manner Hick is going well beyond what ineffability allows.

2. Furthermore, does it make any sense to claim that there is a Real but that no concepts of properties with which we are familiar apply to the Real? What would it mean for an entity to exist without it having *any* substantial properties? An agnostic silence concerning it would seem the only reasonable course. But then why postulate the Real in the first place? How does "There is an X, but X is such that no concepts of substantial properties can be ascribed to it" differ from "There is no X"?

3. Hick's inconsistency is most apparent in his use of the moral criterion (transformation from self-centeredness to Reality-centeredness), both as a reason for postulating the existence of the Real and for discriminating between

legitimate and illegitimate responses to the Real. Hick repeatedly tells us that the Real itself is beyond moral categories such as good and evil.[39] But if the Real is beyond moral categories so that it is neither good nor evil and moral concepts and terms cannot be applied to it, how can "moral transformation" serve as a criterion for an appropriate relationship to the Real? Why suppose that moral transformation within a given religion is at all informative about that tradition's relationship to the Real? Why presume that some behavior is appropriate with respect to the Real but other behavior is not? The Real itself must have moral properties, be a moral being, if the moral criterion is to be used in this manner.

Hick's language about the Real strongly suggests that the Real *is* somehow causally responsible for some of what we see in the various religions and that the Real is a moral being. Thus, despite his efforts to depict the Real in terms which do not privilege any particular religious tradition, Hick tacitly assumes certain theistic characteristics of the Real (intentional action, creation, revelation, moral goodness) even as he states that no such attributes can apply to the Real. Thus Keith Yandell—not inappropriately—characterizes Hick's proposal as "Protestant modernism minus monotheism" or "secularism with incense."[40]

9

DOES GOD
EXIST?

T HERE ARE TWO critical questions confronting any version of religious pluralism: Does an eternal creator God exist? Who is Jesus Christ? The traditional Christian answers to these questions are incompatible with genuine religious pluralism. Religious pluralism makes sense—if it makes sense at all—only on the assumption that there is a pervasive "religious ambiguity" such that theism does not have any stronger rational credentials than non-theistic perspectives. Thus, in defending religious pluralism, Peter Byrne observes,

> The pluralist must, on reasoned grounds, doubt whether the detailed dogmatics of any particular religion can be known with sufficient certainty to enable such a form of religion to be the means of interpreting the whole that is human religion. There is not the certainty in any particular form of religion to enable its world-view to be the basis for a viable interpretation of religion.[41]

Religious ambiguity means that it can be equally rational to interpret the universe as a Christian theist or a Vedantin Hindu or a Theravadin Buddhist would, depending upon one's particular circumstances and experiences.

But why should we accept this assumption about religious ambiguity? The question of God's existence is thus critical to any assessment of religious pluralism. For if there are good reasons for believing that an eternal creator God exists, then there are good reasons for rejecting religions that deny God's existence (e.g., Jainism, Buddhism, some forms of Hinduism) as false. It then becomes impossible to affirm religious pluralism, for if there are compelling grounds for accepting God's existence, then clearly not all religions can be accepted as equally true.

Is it really the case that the proposition "God exists" has no greater evidential or rational support than its denial? To be sure, there is disagreement over the issue of God's existence. But deeply rooted disagreement by itself does not entail that no single perspective is more likely to be true than others nor that all religious perspectives have equal epistemic support. An impressive list of contemporary philosophers have argued persuasively that there are strong reasons for believing that an eternal creator God exists.[42] If they are correct, and I think they are, then religious pluralism should be rejected and theism accepted.

10

WHO IS JESUS?

T HE QUESTION ABOUT the identity of Jesus Christ is also a critical one for religious pluralism. Pluralism requires that Jesus is in principle not significantly different from other religious leaders. If the orthodox Christian understanding of Jesus as found in the New Testament is maintained, then it is impossible to affirm religious pluralism. This is clearly acknowledged by John Hick:

> Traditional orthodoxy says that Jesus of Nazareth was God incarnate—that is, God the Son, the Second Person of a divine Trinity, incarnate—who became man to die for the sins of the world and who founded the church to proclaim this to the ends of the earth, so that all who sincerely take Jesus as their Lord and Savior are justified by his atoning death and will inherit eternal life. It follows from this that Christianity, alone among the world religions, was founded by God in person. ... From this premise it seems obvious that God must wish all human beings to enter this new stream of saved life, so that Christianity shall supersede all the other world faiths. ... Christianity alone is God's own religion, offering a fullness of life that no other tradition

can provide; it is therefore divinely intended for all men and women without exception.[43]

Hick, as we have seen, rejects this view and calls for a radical reinterpretation of Christology in metaphorical terms.

But why should we follow Hick here? Our only substantial access to Jesus' life and teachings is the New Testament, and so it must be the New Testament that controls our understanding of who Jesus is. The comprehensive picture that emerges from the New Testament witness is that God was present and active in Jesus of Nazareth in a way in which he is not elsewhere. There is simply no indication that Jesus is merely one among many other great religious figures. In the language of 2 Corinthians 5:19, God was in Christ reconciling the world to himself, and there is no hint in the Scripture that God was also doing this in other religious leaders and traditions. It is not as though the first-century world was unaware of other religious ways. The idea that there are many alternative paths to the divine with each people or culture having their own distinctive way was common in the first-century Mediterranean world. Had the writers of the New Testament wished to say this, they certainly could have done so. They didn't.

A comprehensive discussion of the New Testament portrayal of Jesus is impossible here, but what follows briefly notes five ways in which Jesus is different from other religious figures.[44]

THE IMPORTANCE OF
JESUS' HISTORICITY

The historicity of the events and sayings attributed to Jesus carries significance for the Christian faith that has no parallel in other religions. In many religions the relevant teachings can be considered independently of the historicity of any particular individual or event.

In 1960, for example, the Protestant theologian Paul Tillich visited Japan, and he asked Buddhist scholars in Kyoto, "If some historian should make it probable that a man of the name Gautama never lived, what would be the consequence for Buddhism?" The Buddhist scholars responded by saying that the question of the historicity of Gautama had never been an issue for Buddhism. "According to the doctrine of Buddhism, the *dharma kaya* [the body of truth] is eternal, and so it does not depend upon the historicity of Gautama."[45] In other words, whether Gautama actually said and did what is ascribed to him does not affect the truth of Buddhist teaching, which transcends historical events. While most Buddhists would insist that the teachings of contemporary Buddhism are consistent with what the historical Gautama taught, they would also acknowledge that the Buddhist *dharma* is eternally true and thus not dependent upon anything in the life of Gautama.

Similarly, in Hinduism the doctrines are regarded as eternal truths that transcend history and thus are not rooted in any particular individual or event. Although Islam takes history seriously, we can still distinguish the truths said to have been revealed by Allah to Muhammad from Muhammad as the particular recipient of this revelation. There is no necessary connection between Muhammad and the revelation; in principle, Allah could have revealed the Qur'an to anyone.

The same cannot be said, however, about Jesus Christ. For Christian faith is inextricably rooted in the historical person of Jesus of Nazareth. Christianity is not merely a collection of inspiring religious teachings; it is based upon God's active intervention in human history. At the center of Christian faith is God's revealing his purposes for the redemption of sinful humanity and providing the means for our salvation through the incarnation in an actual human being, Jesus of Nazareth. It is what Jesus did on the cross and through the resurrection, and not simply what he taught, that makes possible our reconciliation with God. The apostle Paul unambiguously states that if in fact Jesus was not raised from the dead then our faith is futile and useless, and we are still in our sins (1 Cor 15:14–19). The actual resurrection of Jesus Christ from the dead—not merely the inspiring idea of resurrection—is foundational to Christian faith. For the resurrection is God's stamp of approval upon the life and teachings of Jesus, the defeat of death and evil, and the inauguration of a qualitatively new form of life (Rom 1:4; 1 Cor 15:26, 50–58). This distinguishes Christian faith from other religions, such as Buddhism. Whereas it is possible to think of Buddhist teachings apart from the historical life of Gautama, the Christian faith makes no sense apart from the actual life, death, and resurrection of Jesus of Nazareth.

The importance of historicity for Christian faith naturally raises the question about the degree to which we can have confidence that the New Testament writings are at all accurate in what they say about the life and teachings of Jesus. Some complex and controversial issues are involved here, but there are strong reasons for accepting the New Testament witness as a reliable account of Jesus' life, death, and resurrection.[46] While we cannot pursue the issues in depth, we can briefly note one major difference between questions of history and the New Testament as opposed to history and Buddhist sources.

In terms of both the volume and quality of early evidence, we have much greater access to the historical Jesus and the early Christian community than we do to Gautama and the early Buddhist community. There is an abundance of early manuscripts of the New Testament so that we can be confident that what we have in the New Testament today is indeed what the original authors wrote. Craig Blomberg explains,

> Scholars of almost every theological stripe attest to the profound care with which the New Testament books were copied in the Greek language, and later translated and preserved in Syriac, Coptic, Latin and a variety of other ancient European and Middle

Eastern languages. In the original Greek alone, over 5,000 manuscripts and manuscript fragments of portions of the New Testament have been preserved from the early centuries of Christianity. … Overall, 97–99% of the New Testament can be reconstructed beyond any reasonable doubt, and no Christian doctrine is founded solely or even primarily on textually disputed passages.[47]

Moreover, the gap in time between the death of Jesus and the earliest New Testament writings is much smaller than the gap between Gautama's death and the earliest written Buddhist texts. Although there is little question about the fact of Gautama's existence, there is considerable dispute over when he lived, with dates for his death ranging from 480 to 386 BC.[48] The earliest Buddhist scriptures were put into writing in Pali sometime in the first century BC; prior to that time they were transmitted orally.[49] Thus, assuming the Buddha's death at 386 BC and the writing of the Pali texts around 80 BC, we have a gap of some 300 years between Gautama's death and the first Buddhist writings. If the 480 BC date for his death is accepted, then the gap becomes 400 years. Moreover, the early Pali writings consisted largely of instructions for monastic life and sayings, stories and anecdotes of the Buddha and the early disciples; the "biographies" of the Buddha appear even later.

By contrast, the temporal gap between the death of Jesus and the writing of the New Testament is much shorter. It is generally agreed that Jesus was crucified in either

AD 30 or 33.⁵⁰ The apostle Paul's epistles were written between about AD 50 and the late 60s (1 Thessalonians, arguably the earliest of the New Testament letters, was probably written by Paul in AD 50). This leaves a gap of only seventeen to twenty years between Jesus' death and the earliest New Testament writing, with Paul's writings falling within about thirty-five years of Jesus' death. The last of the New Testament books was probably completed around AD 90, leaving about sixty years separating it from the death of Jesus.⁵¹ This, combined with the abundance of manuscript evidence for the text of the New Testament, provides grounds for much greater confidence in the reliability of the New Testament portraits of Jesus than is the case with early Buddhist writings concerning Gautama.

JESUS, UNLIKE SOME RELIGIOUS LEADERS, WAS A MONOTHEIST

Each religious figure must be understood within the historical context of his time. Jesus was a Jew living in a society in which the reality of Yahweh, the one creator God, was assumed. Like his contemporaries, Jesus was a monotheist who accepted the Old Testament perspective that only Yahweh, the God of Israel, is the true God, the creator and ruler of all things. The importance of monotheism is reflected in the Shema: "Hear, O Israel: The LORD our God, the LORD is one" (Deut 6:4). When asked by a religious expert which is the greatest commandment, Jesus answered by quoting the Shema followed by the commands to love God and one's neighbor (Mark 12:28–31). There is no historical evidence that Jesus questioned the existence of God; to the contrary, God's reality is presupposed in all that Jesus says and does.

While some religious leaders, such as Muhammad, are also monotheists, many others are not. There has long been debate over Confucius' views on God or the gods, with some interpreting him as a kind of theist and others regarding him as agnostic on the subject.[52] The Buddha rejected the Brahmanical teachings about the reality of Brahman, the supreme being in Hinduism, and Buddhism has generally been understood as rejecting the idea of a creator God. It is common in the West to regard Buddhism as simply agnostic about God, but this is a misleading recent innovation. Most Buddhist traditions have historically been atheistic. The Sri Lankan Buddhist scholar K. N. Jayatilleke observes that, if by "God" we mean a supreme being and creator, then "the Buddha is an atheist and Buddhism in both its Theravada and Mahayana forms is atheistic. . . . In denying that the universe is a product of a Personal God, who creates it in time and plans a consummation at the end of time, Buddhism is a form of atheism."[53] Paul Williams, a leading scholar of Buddhism and former Buddhist who converted to Roman Catholicism, states,

> Buddhists do not believe in the existence of God. There need be no debating about this. In practicing Buddhism one never finds talk of God, there

is no role for God, and it is not difficult to find in Buddhist texts attacks on the existence of an omnipotent, all-good Creator of the universe.[54]

Thus, one thing distinguishing Jesus from some religious leaders is his clear commitment to the reality of an eternal creator God.

IS THE PROBLEM SIN
OR IGNORANCE?

As we have seen, the major religions all claim that there is some fundamental problem afflicting humankind and the cosmos at large. The religions offer varying diagnoses of this problem and, accordingly, different prescriptions for its cure. According to Jesus, our root problem is sin, the deliberate rejection of God's righteous ways (Mark 7:1–22). It is not ignorance or some cosmic imbalance that causes the human predicament. Rather, it is a corrupt heart or a perverted inner disposition such that "everyone who practices sin is a slave to sin" (John 8:34). Sin, of course, is more than merely moral failure; it must always be understood as an offense against a holy and righteous God. In other words, sin is a concept that makes sense only in a theistic context. Furthermore, although Jesus consistently called others to repentance (Matt 4:17), he never repented for any sin. Not only does Jesus define the human predicament in terms of sin and its consequences, but he assumes the authority to do what only God can do—forgive sins (John 8:46; Mark 2:1–12).

The Buddha, by contrast, diagnosed the root problem as deeply embedded ignorance. Gautama taught that it is ignorance about the true nature of reality—and in particular, about the impermanence of all things and the corollary that there is no enduring person or soul—which results in craving and attachment, and thus the suffering of rebirth. The Buddhist scholar Walpola Rahula says, "There is no 'sin' in Buddhism, as sin is understood in some religions. The root of all evil is ignorance (*avijja*) and false views (*micchaditthi*)."[55] It should not be surprising that we do not find in Buddhism the biblical concept of sin, for in Buddhism there is no holy and righteous God against whom one might sin. Other Indian religions such as Hinduism and Jainism also locate the fundamental problem as one of ignorance, although they disagree over the nature of this ignorance.

THE NEW TESTAMENT PRESENTS JESUS CHRIST AS GOD INCARNATE, FULLY MAN AND FULLY GOD

Christians maintain that the comprehensive witness of the New Testament is that in the human person of Jesus of Nazareth, the one eternal God assumed human nature: God became incarnate in Jesus, fully God and fully man. The incarnation forms the apex of God's self-revelation to humankind.

The Letter to the Hebrews states, "Long ago, at many times and in many ways, God spoke to our fathers by the prophets, but in these last days he has spoken to us by his Son, whom he appointed the heir of all things, through whom also he created the world" (Heb 1:1–2). The Gospel of John identifies Jesus with the preexistent Word (the Logos), who "was with God and who was God" and through whom "all things were made," and it then asserts that "the Word became flesh and made his dwelling among us" (John 1:1–4, 14). Throughout the New Testament, sometimes explicitly but often implicitly, Jesus is placed in an unprecedented relationship of identity with Yahweh, the everlasting creator God of the Old Testament. Jesus is presented as claiming the authority to do things that only God can do, such as forgive sins (Mark 2:5–11); judge the world (Matt 19:28; 25:31–46); give life, even to the dead (John 5:21, 25–29; 11:17–44). Jesus states that anyone who has seen him has seen the Father (John 14:9)—a remarkable claim in the context of Jewish monotheism. Jesus identifies himself with the "I AM" of Exodus 3:14 and in so doing is understood by his contemporaries to be identifying himself with God (John 8:58). The apostle Paul asserts that all of the "fullness" (*pleroma*) of God is present in the human person of Jesus: "In him all the fullness of God was pleased to dwell" (Col 1:19; 2:9). Understood within the context of first-century Jewish monotheism, the assertion that in Jesus of Nazareth the one eternal God has become man is unique in its audacity and is unparalleled in other religions.

It is sometimes said that Jesus himself never taught anything like the orthodox Christian teaching on the incarnation and that this was a much later doctrinal innovation of the Christian church. The human Jesus, originally regarded by his followers as just a great teacher and perhaps even the Messiah, over time became revered as more than merely a man, resulting, under Greek influence, in the metaphysical conceptions of him as Son of God, God the Son, and finally the Second Person of the Holy Trinity in the sophisticated Trinitarian formula.

There is much that could be said by way of response to this claim, but we will confine ourselves to two related points. First, there simply is not sufficient time during the writing of the New Testament for such a dramatic evolution in understanding the significance of Jesus. Second, while some development within the New Testament writings themselves can be traced, the "high Christology" that identifies Jesus with Yahweh, God the creator, is actually found in the earliest evidence we have of Christian belief and practice.

As noted above, all the writings of the New Testament were completed by about AD 90 (most considerably earlier) so that at most there is a gap of some sixty years between the death of Jesus and the completion of the last book of the New Testament. This is not sufficient time for a radical evolution from the view that Jesus is just an extraordinary man to that of him as in fact God-the-creator-become-man. New Testament scholar C. F. D. Moule maintains that the suggestion that such "high" Christology evolved from a primitive "low" Christology by a gradual process over time simply does not fit the data. To the contrary, he argues, the transition from invoking Jesus as revered master to the acclamation of him as divine Lord is best understood as a development in understanding according to which "the various estimates of Jesus reflected in the New Testament [are], in essence, only attempts to describe what was already there from the beginning. They are not successive additions of something new, but only the drawing out and articulating of what is there." Moule claims, "Jesus was, *from the beginning,* such a one as appropriately to be described in the ways in which, sooner or later, he did come to be described in the New Testament period—for instance, as 'Lord' and even, in some sense, as 'God.'"[56] Some of the most elevated Christology and clearest affirmations of the deity of Christ are in the Pauline epistles, widely accepted as the earliest documents in the New Testament (see Rom 9:5; Phil 2:5–11; Col 1:15–17, 19; 2:9).

One way to determine early perspectives on Christology is to examine not only the language the New Testament uses in reference to Jesus but also the practices of the early Christian community. Larry Hurtado has demonstrated that Christian worship of Jesus is presupposed by the earliest New Testament writings and thus that the practice of worshiping Jesus as divine by his early followers—most of whom were Jewish—is even earlier than these writings.[57] Hurtado claims that within the first couple of decades of the Christian movement, "Jesus was treated as a recipient of religious devotion and was associated with God in striking ways."[58] He states,

> The origins of the worship of Jesus are so early that practically any evolutionary approach is rendered invalid as historical explanation. Our earliest Christian writings, from approximately 50–60 CE, already presuppose cultic devotion to Jesus as a familiar and defining feature of Christian circles wherever they were found (1 Cor. 1:2).[59]

Furthermore, Hurtado maintains,

> This intense devotion to Jesus, which includes reverencing him as divine, was offered and articulated characteristically within a firm stance of exclusivist monotheism, particularly in the circles of early Christians that anticipated and helped to establish what became mainstream (and subsequently, familiar) Christianity.[60]

JESUS TEACHES HE IS THE WAY TO SALVATION

As we have seen, it is possible with some religions to separate the religion's teachings from the historical events in the life of the religion's founder. This is the case, for example, with Gautama and Buddhism. Moreover, there is within the teachings attributed to the Buddha a strong sense of each individual being responsible for his or her own liberation.

The Buddha did proclaim the *dharma*, the teaching leading to liberation, and in this way he can be said to assist all sentient beings. But it is up to each person to grasp the *dharma*, to act upon it, and thereby to attain *nirvana*.[61] Rahula puts it this way: "If the Buddha is to be called a 'saviour' at all, it is only in the sense that he discovered and showed the Path to Liberation, Nirvana. But we must tread the Path ourselves."[62] Much of Buddhism teaches "self-effort" in attaining liberation.

But with Jesus the situation is different. According to the Christian Scriptures, we cannot save ourselves; we are utterly helpless and hopeless apart from the grace of God and the atoning work of Jesus Christ on the cross for us (Eph 2:1–10; Rom 3:9–28). Jesus is consistently presented in the New Testament as the one Savior for all people in all cultures (John 3:16; Acts 2:37–39; 4:12; Rom 3:21–25; 1 Tim 2:5–6). Jesus called upon others to believe in him and to find salvation in him (John 5:24; 6:35–58). Jesus does not merely teach the way—he claims to be the way to the Father (John 14:6). It is not simply that Jesus has discovered the truth and that if we follow his teachings we too can find the way for ourselves. The Buddha can be understood as saying, "Follow my teachings, follow the dharma and you too can experience the way leading to enlightenment." But Jesus claims much more than simply that he has discovered the way to the Father and that if we follow his teachings we too can find the way. He puts himself forward as the very embodiment of the way and the truth and the source of life. It is because of who he is and what he has done for us on the cross and in the resurrection that he is himself the way, the truth, and the life. Thus, the truth of Jesus' teachings cannot be separated from the ontological grounding of this truth in the person of Christ as the incarnate Word of God.

11

AN EVANGELICAL THEOLOGY OF RELIGIONS

WE HAVE SEEN that religious pluralism is inadequate as a general theory about the relationship among the religions. Not only does it suffer from internal inconsistencies, but it is incompatible with Christian commitments concerning the reality of God and the person of Jesus Christ. But if religious pluralism is to be rejected, how should Christians think about other religions? What theological principles should guide us in our approach to religious diversity? Christians maintain that the eternal creator God has spoken to humankind in an intelligible manner in the incarnation and the written Scriptures. Thus, in thinking about other religions, we are to submit to God's revelation as truth, allowing it to control our beliefs even when this truth may not be particularly palatable to contemporary tastes.

Thinking theologically about other religions involves us in what is sometimes called the theology of religions. Veli-Matti Kärkkäinen defines theology of religions as

> that discipline of theological studies which attempts to account theologically for the meaning and value of other religions. Christian theology of religions attempts to think theologically about what it means

for Christians to live with people of other faiths and about the relationship of Christianity to other religions.[63]

A theology of religions must address two basic questions: First, how do we explain theologically the sheer fact of human religiosity? Why are people incurably religious? Second, how do we account theologically for the particularities of religious expression, the many diverse beliefs and practices we find among the religious traditions? Both similarities and differences between Christianity and other religions are to be explained theologically. An evangelical theology of religions should be shaped by four major biblical themes: creation, general revelation, sin, and demonic influence.[64]

CREATION AND GENERAL REVELATION

The religions, in varying degrees, do manifest elements of truth, goodness, and beauty. The Confucian *Analects*, for example, based upon the sayings of Confucius some five centuries before the time of Christ, contains two statements of the Golden Rule.[65] At a more basic level, it is because God has created human beings with certain dispositions and capacities that we find among humankind the capacity for religious expression, the recognition of a reality transcending the physical world, the yearning for the Creator and life beyond physical death, the acknowledgement that the world as we experience it is not the way it is supposed to be, and the search for ways in which to appease God or the gods and to attain a better existence. Scripture teaches that human beings are created in God's image (Gen 9:6; 1 Cor 11:7; Jas 3:9) and that God has revealed something of himself and what he expects from humankind in a general manner through the universe and the human person, especially the human conscience (Ps 19:1–4; Acts 14:15–17; 17:22–31; Rom 1:18–32; 2:14–15). The fact that all human beings are created in God's image with a rudimentary awareness of God's reality and our obligation to him, as well as the biblical themes of God's general revelation throughout the created order, help to explain the commonalities that we see between Christian faith and other religions.

SIN

But religious expression also includes much that is false, idolatrous, and a perversion of God's creation and revelation. Thus, the biblical emphasis upon human sin and rebellion against God (Gen 2:16–17; 3:1–24; Rom 5:12) is critical for a theology of religions, for this accounts for the fact that we find in the religions not only goodness but also much that is profoundly evil. Sin is a pervasive corruption of the human heart, and it affects all aspects of our being. All people are sinners. There is no one who is naturally righteous before God and consistently does what is right

(Ps 14:2–3; Isa 53:6; Rom 3:10–18, 23). Sin is both personal and social in its manifestation, and it is found both in the individual and collectively in cultures and societies. Not surprisingly then, the impact of sin is evident in the religions as well as in other dimensions of life.

DEMONIC INFLUENCE

Finally, while it would be simplistic to attribute all of the phenomena of the religions to the influence of demonic powers, it would be equally naive to pretend that the Adversary, Satan, is not active through the religions. The demonic is present in other religions just as it is active in the many domains of life. The apostle Paul reminded his readers that the pagan sacrifices of Corinthian religion, which seemed rather innocent to some, were in reality offered to demons (1 Cor 10:20).

Religions are complex phenomena that include, in any particular case, varying degrees of truth and goodness along with much falsehood and evil. Chris Wright captures this dialectic when he says,

> The fallen duplicity of man is that he *simultaneously* seeks after God his Maker and flees from God his Judge. Man's religions, therefore, *simultaneously* manifest both these human tendencies. This is what makes a simplistic verdict on other religions— whether blandly positive or wholly negative—so unsatisfactory and indeed unbiblical.[66]

But to the extent that they distort God's truth as revealed in Scripture and lead people to place their trust in anything apart from the living God, the religions, like anything else that has this effect, are to be rejected as idolatrous.

12

SALVATION: WHAT ABOUT THOSE WHO NEVER HEAR ABOUT JESUS?

ACCORDING TO THE Scriptures, salvation is a gift of God's grace, is based upon the person and work of Jesus Christ on the cross, and comes through an exercise of faith in God (Rom 3:25; 2 Cor 5:18–19, 21; Heb 2:17; 1 John 2:2; 4:10). Salvation is totally the work of God's grace and is not the result of human effort or good works (Eph 2:8–10). The Bible maintains that Jesus is the unique, only Savior for all of humankind; no one is reconciled to God except through Jesus Christ (John 3:16, 36; 14:6; Acts 4:12; 1 Tim 2:5).

The emphasis upon Jesus Christ as the only Savior naturally raises questions about the scope of salvation and the destiny of those who do not hear the gospel of Jesus Christ. While this is a sensitive issue, we must form our conclusions on the basis of what Scripture clearly teaches and be careful to avoid unhealthy speculation beyond what Scripture affirms. Evangelical Christians generally agree that the biblical witness is clear on the following points:

1. All peoples in all cultures, including sincere followers of other religions, are sinners and face God's just condemnation for sin.

2. Salvation—that is, forgiveness of sin, justification and reconciliation with God, and all that this implies—is available only on the

basis of the sinless person and atoning work of Jesus Christ. All who are saved are saved only through Jesus Christ.

3. No one is saved merely by being sincere, or by doing good works, or by being devout and pious in following a particular religion.

4. Salvation is always only by God's grace and must be personally accepted through faith.

5. Ultimately, not everyone will be saved. Some, probably many, will be eternally lost.

6. God is entirely righteous, just, and fair in his dealings with humankind. No one who is condemned by God is condemned unjustly.

7. Both out of a sense of obedience to her Lord and compassion for the lost, the church must be actively engaged in making disciples of all peoples, including sincere adherents of other religions. Moreover, most agree that the clear pattern in the New Testament is that people first hear the gospel and then, through the work of the Holy Spirit, respond in faith to the proclamation of the Word and are saved.

But is it nevertheless possible for some who have never heard the gospel of Jesus Christ to be saved? There is some disagreement among evangelicals on the question of the unevangelized, with evangelical responses falling into three broad categories. The differences between these positions does not concern the *means* of salvation (grace versus works) but rather the amount of knowledge necessary for a saving response to God.[67]

Many evangelicals hold that only those who hear the gospel and explicitly respond in faith to the name of Jesus in this life can be saved. Explicit knowledge of the gospel of Jesus Christ is thus essential for salvation, and there is no hope for those who die without having heard the gospel.[68]

A rather different perspective is that of the "wider hope," which maintains that we can expect that large numbers of those who have never heard the gospel will nevertheless be saved. Although Jesus Christ is the one Savior for all people and salvation is possible only because of Christ's atoning work on the cross, one need not know explicitly about Jesus Christ and the cross to be saved.[69]

Other evangelicals, however, find themselves somewhere between these two positions, convinced that each of the above views goes beyond what the biblical data affirm. Those in this group are willing to admit in principle that God might save some who have never explicitly heard the gospel, but they add that we simply do not know whether this occurs or, if so, how many might be saved in this manner. John Stott, for example, states that on the basis of Scripture, we know that

Jesus Christ is the only Saviour, and that salvation is by God's grace alone, on the ground of Christ's cross alone, and by faith alone. The only question, therefore, is how much knowledge and understanding of the gospel people need before they can cry to God for mercy and be saved. In the Old Testament people were "justified by faith" even though they had little knowledge or expectation of Christ. Perhaps there are others today in a similar position, who know that they are guilty before God and that they cannot do anything to win his favour, but who in self-despair call upon the God they dimly perceive to save them. If God saves such, as many evangelical Christians believe, their salvation is still only through Christ, only by faith.[70]

Those embracing this view maintain that some knowledge of God, our sinfulness, and our inability to save ourselves is necessary, but they hold that such minimal knowledge may be available through general revelation to those who have not yet heard the gospel.

Perhaps the wisest response to the issue is to acknowledge the possibility that some who never hear the gospel might nonetheless, through God's grace, respond to what they know of God through general revelation and turn to him in faith for forgiveness. But to speculate about how many, if any, are saved in this manner is to go beyond what the Scriptures affirm. Millard Erickson observes, "There are no unambiguous instances in Scripture of persons who became true believers through responding to general revelation alone. Scripture does not indicate how many, if any, come to salvation that way."[71] The pattern in the New Testament is for people to hear the gospel of Jesus Christ and then to respond by God's grace to the gospel in saving faith.

13

LIVING
AMONG
RELIGIOUS
OTHERS

W E MUST REMEMBER that in the theology of religions, we are not dealing merely with abstract systems or beliefs but with real people who live in certain religious ways. What does it mean to be a disciple of Jesus Christ in a world of religious diversity? How should followers of Christ respond to religious others? How do Christians acknowledge Jesus Christ as Lord of all of life in modern, democratic societies increasingly characterized by religious diversity and that are committed to protection of freedom of religious and non-religious expression? The issues here are complex and require proper navigation of two sets of obligations: our responsibilities as disciples of Jesus Christ and as good citizens.

THE GREAT COMMISSION: MAKE DISCIPLES

It is helpful to approach these questions in light of two specific instructions from our Lord. The first is the so-called Great Commission, given just prior to Christ's ascension:

> And Jesus came and said to them, "All authority in heaven and on earth has been given to me. Go therefore and make disciples of all nations, baptizing them in the name of the Father and of the Son

and of the Holy Spirit, teaching them to observe all that I have commanded you. And behold, I am with you always, to the end of the age." (Matt 28:18–20)

As followers of Jesus Christ, we are to "make disciples" of all people. Faithfulness to our Lord and compassion for the lost requires that we share the gospel of Jesus Christ with all people—including sincere followers of other religions—urging them to embrace Jesus as their Lord and Savior. Disciple-making thus includes evangelism, although it involves much more than just sharing the gospel with others.

Evangelism is controversial today, as many Christians feel that there is something inappropriate about trying to persuade sincere followers of other religions to change their commitments and embrace the Christian gospel. This is often linked to a certain embarrassment over the modern missionary movement, which is often dismissed today as simply the religious side of Western imperialism. But the Christian gospel is inherently missionary. It is good news of reconciliation with God that must be shared with a world that is desperately lost. The missionary statesman Lesslie Newbigin correctly links the recent discomfiture over missions with a lack of confidence in the biblical picture of Jesus Christ:

> The contemporary embarrassment about the missionary movement of the previous century is not, as we like to think, evidence that we have become

more humble. It is, I fear, much more clearly evidence of a shift in belief. It is evidence that we are less ready to affirm the uniqueness, the centrality, the decisiveness of Jesus Christ as universal Lord and Savior, the Way by following whom the world is to find its true goal, the Truth by which every other claim to truth is to be tested, the Life in whom alone life in its fullness is to be found.[72]

Similarly, the Dutch missiologist Johannes Verkuyl remarks, "The subversion of the missionary mandate one encounters in various contemporary missiologies and models of theology of religion must simply be called what it is: betrayal of Jesus Christ."[73] The issue, then, is not whether we engage in evangelism with religious others, but rather how we do so.

THE GREAT COMMANDMENT:
LOVE GOD AND YOUR NEIGHBOR

This leads us to the second of Jesus' instructions for his followers, the so-called Great Commandment.

And one of them, a lawyer, asked him a question to test him. "Teacher, which is the great commandment in the Law?" And he said to him, "You shall love the Lord your God with all your heart and with all your soul and with all your mind. This is the great and first commandment. And a second is like it: You shall love your neighbor as yourself. On these two commandments depend all the Law and the Prophets." (Matt 22:35–40; compare Deut 6:4–5; Mark 12:28–34; Luke 10:25–37)

As Christ's disciples, we are to love God with our entire being and to love our neighbor—including religious others—as we love ourselves.

What does it mean to love our neighbor? How do we love religious others with whom we come into contact? Among other things, surely this means accepting Muslims, Hindus, and Buddhists as fellow human beings created by God and bearing the divine image, treating them with dignity and respect, and seeking their welfare. It includes building relationships with them and, to the extent that we are able, meeting their needs. On occasion it might also mean defending their rights and ensuring justice on their behalf.

Part of what drives the agenda for religious pluralism in the West today is the widespread perception that any form of "religious exclusivism" undermines harmonious religious coexistence. Only ideological pluralism, it is said, can provide the framework for peaceful religious diversity. Monotheistic religions—especially Christianity—are regarded as contributing to the problem of religious tensions, not part of the solution. The church must take these perceptions seriously and show a skeptical world that Christians can be strongly committed to Jesus Christ while also working to promote peaceful relations among religions. Christians must take the lead and demonstrate through concrete actions that we do accept in appropriate ways the ethnic, cultural, and religious diversity in the West. But at the same time, we cannot abandon our commitment to Jesus Christ as the one Lord and Savior for all peoples. So even as we accept Buddhists and Muslims as fellow human beings created in God's image, we must also urge them to be reconciled to God by acknowledging Jesus Christ as their Lord and Savior.

Acknowledgments

THE SERIES Questions for Restless Minds is produced by the Christ on Campus Initiative, under the stewardship of the editorial board of D. A. Carson (senior editor), Douglas Sweeney, Graham Cole, Dana Harris, Thomas McCall, Geoffrey Fulkerson, and Scott Manetsch. The editorial board recognizes with gratitude the many outstanding evangelical authors who have contributed to this series, as well as the sponsorship of Trinity Evangelical Divinity School (Deerfield, Illinois), and the financial support of the MAC Foundation and the Carl F. H. Henry Center for Theological Understanding. The editors also wish to thank Christopher Gow, who created the study questions accompanying each book, and Todd Hains, our editor at Lexham Press. May God alone receive the glory for this endeavor!

Study Guide Questions

1. Netland starts by defining "religious pluralism" in two ways; what are the two different meanings of this phrase?

2. Netland says that religious pluralism is attractive to our culture; why do you think that is?

3. What are some truth claims that Christians make that are incompatible with Hinduism? Buddhism? Islam?

4. Netland makes the case that, "If the orthodox Christian understanding of Jesus as found in the New Testament is maintained, then it is impossible to affirm religious pluralism" (79). Do you agree with his reasoning? Why or why not?

5. What makes Jesus different from other faith leaders?

6. How would you summarize a Christian "theology of religions"?

7. Review Netland's recommendations about loving people of other faith. What is a practical way you could show love to your neighbors of different faiths this week?

For Further Reading

Carson, D. A. *The Gagging of God: Christianity Confronts Pluralism.* Zondervan, 1996.

A comprehensive and thorough discussion of the many biblical and theological issues involved in religious pluralism by a leading evangelical New Testament scholar and theologian. Essential reading for anyone desiring a biblically responsible approach to religious pluralism.

Edwards, James R. *Is Jesus the Only Savior?* Eerdmans, 2005.

A helpful examination of the New Testament understanding of Jesus Christ in light of the questions raised by pluralism and radical scholarship. Vigorously defends Jesus as the only Savior of the world.

Erickson, Millard. *How Shall They Be Saved? The Destiny of Those Who Do Not Hear of Jesus*. Baker, 1996.

> A leading evangelical theologian provides a clear and comprehensive discussion of the conditions for salvation in Scripture. Carefully examines various views on the question of the unevangelized.

Griffiths, Paul. *Problems of Religious Diversity*. Blackwell, 2001.

> A helpful introduction to the many philosophical issues in religious pluralism by a Christian analytic philosopher who is also an expert in Buddhism. Although the discussion is primarily philosophical, the issues addressed are relevant to the theology of religions.

Kärkkäinen, Veli-Matti. *An Introduction to the Theology of Religions: Biblical, Historical and Contemporary Perspectives*. IVP, 2003.

> A very helpful general overview of the subject of theology of religions, as well as a broad survey of the many thinkers and positions found in the current debates. Primarily descriptive, without arguing for a particular view on theology of religions.

Netland, Harold. *Encountering Religious Pluralism: The Challenge to Christian Faith and Mission.* IVP, 2001.

An examination of the issues in the current debates over Christian faith and other religions as well as a critique of the religious pluralism of John Hick.

Okholm, Dennis L. and Timothy R. Phillips, eds. *Four Views on Salvation in a Pluralistic World.* Zondervan, 1996.

An interesting exchange between John Hick, Clark Pinnock, Alister McGrath, R. Douglas Geivett, and W. Gary Phillips over the question of the relation of Christian faith to other religions. Clearly presents differences between the various positions.

Notes

1. For background on the parable of the ring, see Alan Mittleman, "Toleration, Liberty, and Truth: A Parable," *Harvard Theological Review* 95.4 (2002): 353–72.

2. Gotthold Ephraim Lessing, *Nathan the Wise*, trans. Patrick Maxwell, ed. George Alexander Kohut (Bloch, 1939), 243.

3. Lessing, *Nathan the Wise*, 249.

4. Lessing, *Nathan the Wise*, 252–53.

5. Joann O'Brien and Martin Palmer, *The Atlas of Religion: Mapping Contemporary Challenges and Beliefs* (University of California Press, 2007), 14.

6. Ninian Smart and Frederick Denny, eds., *Atlas of the World's Religions*, 2nd ed. (Oxford University Press, 2007), 15.

7. See Christopher Partridge, ed., *New Religions: A Guide: New Religious Movements, Sects and Alternative Spiritualities* (Oxford University Press, 2004).

8. Robert Wilken, *Remembering the Christian Past* (Eerdmans, 1995), 27, 42.

9.   For a survey of different perspectives on other reli-
      gions, see Veli-Matti Kärkkäinen, *An Introduction
      to the Theology of Religions: Biblical, Historical and
      Contemporary Perspectives* (IVP, 2003).

10.   Peter Berger, *A Far Glory: The Quest for Faith in
      an Age of Credulity* (Anchor, 1992), 67, 146–47
      (emphasis in original).

11.   Robert Wuthnow, *America and the Challenges of
      Religious Diversity* (Princeton University Press,
      2005), 191.

12.   Peter Byrne, "It Is Not Reasonable to Believe
      That Only One Religion Is True," in *Contemporary
      Debates in Philosophy of Religion*, ed. Michael L.
      Peterson and Raymond J. Vanarragon (Blackwell,
      2003), 204.

13.   On Hick's theological journey, see John Hick, *John
      Hick: An Autobiography* (Oneworld, 2002), and
      Harold Netland, *Encountering Religious Pluralism:
      The Challenge to Christian Faith and Mission* (IVP,
      2001), 158–77.

14.   John Hick, *A Christian Theology of Religions: The
      Rainbow of Faiths* (Westminster John Knox, 1995),
      27.

15.   John Hick, *The Fifth Dimension* (Oneworld, 1999),
      77.

16.   John Hick, *An Interpretation of Religion: Human
      Responses to the Transcendent*, 2nd ed. (Yale Univer-
      sity Press, 2004), 8.

17. Hick, *An Interpretation of Religion*, 350.

18. Hick, *A Christian Theology of Religions*, 69.

19. John Hick, *Problems of Religious Pluralism* (St. Martin's, 1985), 86–87.

20. John Hick, "Jesus and the World Religions," in *The Myth of God Incarnate*, ed. John Hick (Westminster John Knox, 1977), 172 (emphasis in original).

21. John Hick, *God Has Many Names* (Westminster John Knox, 1980), 74.

22. John Hick, *The Metaphor of God Incarnate: Christology in a Pluralistic Age* (Westminster John Knox, 1993), 98.

23. Roger Schmidt, et al., *Patterns of Religion* (Wadsworth, 1999), 10.

24. Ninian Smart, *The Religious Experience*, 5th ed. (Prentice-Hall, 1996), 1–8; Smart, *Worldviews: Crosscultural Explorations of Human Beliefs*, 2nd ed. (Charles Scribners Sons, 1995).

25. Smart, *The Religious Experience of Mankind*, 5.

26. The Four Noble Truths, which are said to have been expressed in the Buddha's first sermon and comprise the heart of classical Buddhist teaching, are as follows: (1) All of existence is characterized by *dukkha* (usually translated as "suffering" or "dissatisfaction"). (2) There are discernible causes of suffering, and the root cause is *tanha* (desire, thirst, or craving). (3) The disease of suffering is curable, and when desire/craving cease, suffering ceases as

well. (4) The cessation of desire/craving (and thus suffering) is achieved through following the Noble Eightfold Path, which is a series of highly disciplined steps that lead to enlightenment. They are clustered into three general categories: proper view (right understanding and right thought), proper conduct (right speech, right action, right livelihood), and proper practice (right effort, right mindfulness, and right concentration). See Donald W. Mitchell, *Buddhism: Introducing the Buddhist Experience*, 2nd ed. (Oxford University Press, 2008), 49–61.

27. Keith Yandell, "How to Sink in Cognitive Quicksand: Nuancing Religious Pluralism," in *Contemporary Debates in Philosophy of Religion*, 191.

28. Although the meaning of "truth" in religion is the same as that of "truth" in other domains, the ways in which we determine whether a given religious belief is true will of course be somewhat different from ways in which we determine truth in, say, physics or history.

29. K. N. Jayatilleke, *The Message of the Buddha*, ed. Ninian Smart (Free Press, 1974), 43–44.

30. Hajime Nakamura, "Unity and Diversity in Buddhism," in *The Path of the Buddha: Buddhism Interpreted by Buddhists*, ed. Kenneth W. Morgan (Ronald, 1956), 372. See also Paul Griffiths, "Philosophizing Across Cultures: or, How to Argue With a Buddhist," *Criterion* 26 (Winter

1987), 10–14; Griffiths, *An Apology for Apologetics: A Study in the Logic of Interreligious Dialogue* (Orbis, 1991); and Keith Yandell, "Religious Traditions and Rational Assessments," in *The Routledge Companion to Philosophy of Religion*, ed. Chad Meister and Paul Copan (Routledge, 2007), 204–15.

31. See Netland, *Encountering Religious Pluralism*, 293–97.

32. See Richard King, *Indian Philosophy: An Introduction to Hindu and Buddhist Thought* (Georgetown University Press, 1999).

33. *The Vedanta Sutras of Badarayanna with the Commentary of Sankara*, trans. George Thibaut (1896; repr., Dover, 1962), 2:399.

34. "Jaina Sutras" in *Sacred Books of the East*, trans. Hermann Jacobi, ed. F. Max Muller (Richmond, Surrey, 2001), 45:418.

35. H. H. The XIVth Dalai Lama, "'Religious Harmony' and The Bodhgaya Interviews," in *Christianity Through Non-Christian Eyes*, ed. Paul J. Griffiths (Orbis, 1990), 169.

36. Hick, *A Christian Theology of Religions*, 27.

37. See Keith Yandell, *Philosophy of Religion* (Routledge, 1999), 71–72.

38. See Hick, *A Christian Theology of Religions*, 27, 60, 63, 67.

39. John Hick, "Ineffability," *Religious Studies* 36 (March 2000): 44.

40. Keith Yandell, "How to Sink in Cognitive Quicksand," 194, and "Revisiting Religious Pluralism," *Christian Scholar's Review* 31.3 (Spring 2002): 319.

41. Byrne, "It Is Not Reasonable to Believe That Only One Religion Is True," 204.

42. For helpful discussions of arguments for God's existence, see Richard Swinburne, *The Existence of God* 2nd ed. (Oxford University Press, 2004); Swinburne, *Is There A God?* (Oxford University Press, 1996); Stephen T. Davis, *God, Reason and Theistic Proofs* (Eerdmans, 1997); Keith Yandell, *Philosophy of Religion*, 167–235; and Chad Meister and Paul Copan, eds., *The Routledge Companion to the Philosophy of Religion* (Routledge, 2007), 329–93.

43. John Hick, "A Pluralist View," in *Four Views on Salvation in a Pluralistic World*, ed. Dennis L. Okholm and Timothy R. Phillips (Zondervan, 1996), 51–52.

44. For a helpful discussion of the biblical data on Jesus as these relate to issues of religious pluralism, see James R. Edwards, *Is Jesus the Only Savior?* (Eerdmans, 2005).

45. See Robert W. Wood, ed., "Tillich Encounters Japan," *Japanese Religions* 2 (May 1961), 48–71.

46. See Craig L. Blomberg, *Who Is Jesus of Nazareth?* (Lexham Press, 2021). For helpful introductions to the issues of history, the New Testament, and Christian faith, see Colin Brown, "Historical Jesus, Quest of," in *Dictionary of Jesus and the Gospels*,

ed. Joel B. Green, Scot McKnight, and I. Howard
Marshall (IVP, 1992), 326–41; Craig Blomberg, *The
Historical Reliability of the Gospels*, 2nd ed. (IVP,
2007); Paul Barnett, *Is the New Testament Reliable?*,
2nd ed. (IVP, 2003); and Craig A. Evans, *Fabricat-
ing Jesus: How Modern Scholars Distort the Gospels*
(IVP, 2006).

47. Craig Blomberg, "The Historical Reliability of the
New Testament," in William Lane Craig, *Reason-
able Faith: Christian Faith and Apologetics*, 2nd ed.
(Crossway, 1994), 194–95.

48. On historical issues concerning Gautama the
Buddha, see Donald W. Mitchell, *Buddhism: Intro-
ducing the Buddhist Experience*, 2nd ed. (Oxford
University Press, 2008), 9–32; Hajime Nakamura,
*Gotama Buddha: A Biography Based on the Most
Reliable Texts*, vol. 1, trans. Gaynor Sekimori
(Kosei, 2000); and David Edward Shaner, "Biog-
raphies of the Buddha," *Philosophy East and West* 37
(July 1987): 306–22.

49. See Mitchell, *Buddhism*, 66.

50. On issues relating to the year of Jesus' death, see
Joel B. Green, "Death of Jesus," in *Dictionary of
Jesus and the Gospels*, 148–49.

51. For further discussion on dates and related issues
for each New Testament book, see D.A. Carson
and Douglas J. Moo, *An Introduction to the New
Testament*, 2nd ed. (Zondervan, 2005).

52. See, for example, Julia Ching, *Confucianism and Christianity: A Comparative Study* (Kodansha International, 1977).

53. K. N. Jayatilleke, *The Message of the Buddha*, ed. Ninian Smart (Free Press, 1974), 105.

54. Paul Williams, *The Unexpected Way: On Converting From Buddhism to Catholicism* (T&T Clark, 2002), 25. For more on Buddhist critiques of theism, see Gunapala Dharmasiri, *A Buddhist Critique of the Christian Concept of God* (Golden Leaves, 1988); and Paul Williams, "Aquinas Meets the Buddhists: Prolegomenon to an Authentically Thomas-ist Basis for Dialogue," in *Aquinas in Dialogue: Thomas for the Twenty-First Century*, ed. James Fodor and Christian Bauerschmidt (Blackwell, 2004), 87–117.

55. Walpola Rahula, *What the Buddha Taught* (Grove Press, 1974), 3.

56. C. F. D. Moule, *The Origin of Christology* (Cambridge University Press, 1977), 2–4 (emphasis in the original).

57. Larry W. Hurtado, *Lord Jesus Christ: Devotion to Jesus in Earliest Christianity* (Eerdmans, 2003); and Hurtado, *How on Earth Did Jesus Become a God? Historical Questions about Earliest Devotion to Jesus* (Eerdmans, 2005).

58. Larry Hurtado, *Lord Jesus Christ*, 2. As indicators of such worship, he points to the practices of call-

ing upon the name of the Lord Jesus Christ when believers gathered together (1 Cor 1:2); the use of hymns about or to Jesus as regular parts of Christian worship (Phil 2:5–11); prayer to God "through" Jesus (Rom 1:8), and direct prayer to Jesus himself (Acts 7:59–60; 2 Cor 12:8–9; 1 Thess 3:11–13; 2 Thess 2:16–17); use of the formula "Marana tha!" ("O Lord, Come!") as a prayer in worship (1 Cor 16:22); invoking Jesus' name in healing and exorcism (Acts 3:16; 16:18) as well as in baptism (Acts 2:38); and the celebration of the "Lord's Supper" (1 Cor 11:17–34).

59. Larry Hurtado, *How on Earth Did Jesus Become a God?* (Eerdmans, 2005), 25.

60. Hurtado, *How on Earth Did Jesus Become a God?*, 3. See also Richard Bauckham, *God Crucified: Monotheism and Christology in the New Testament* (Eerdmans, 1998).

61. There are some striking exceptions to this pattern in Mahayana Buddhism, in which various *bodhisattvas* and *buddhas* are said to assist human beings in the pursuit of enlightenment and liberation. The Pure Land tradition, in particular, teaches that we cannot attain enlightenment and rebirth in the Pure Land through our own efforts and that we must rely solely upon the merit and "grace" of the Amida Buddha for such liberation.

62. Rahula, *What the Buddha Taught*, 1–2.

63. Kärkkäinen, *An Introduction to the Theology of Religions*, 20.

64. For further discussion of these points, see Netland, *Encountering Religious Pluralism*, 308–48. See also Winfried Corduan, *A Tapestry of Faiths: The Common Threads Between Christianity and World Religions* (IVP, 2002) and Ida Glaser, *The Bible and Other Faiths: Christian Responsibility in a World of Religions* (IVP, 2005).

65. *Confucius: The Analects*, 12:2 and 15:24, trans. D.C. Lau (Penguin, 1979), 112, 135.

66. Christopher J. H. Wright, "The Christian and Other Religions: The Biblical Evidence," *Themelios* 9.2 (1984): 5.

67. For helpful discussions of the relevant biblical and theological issues in the debate, see D. A. Carson, *The Gagging of God: Christianity Confronts Pluralism* (Zondervan, 1996) and Millard J. Erickson, *How Shall They Be Saved? The Destiny of Those Who Do Not Hear of Jesus* (Baker, 1996).

68. See John Piper, *Let the Nations Be Glad! The Supremacy of God in Missions*, 2nd ed. (Baker, 2003); Ronald Nash, *Is Jesus the Only Savior?* (Zondervan, 1994); and Christopher W. Morgan and Robert A. Peterson, eds., *Faith Comes By Hearing: A Response to Inclusivism* (IVP, 2008).

69. See John Sanders, *No Other Name: An Investigation into the Destiny of the Unevangelized* (Eerdmans, 1992); Clark Pinnock, *A Wideness in God's Mercy: The Finality of Jesus Christ in a World of Religions* (Zondervan, 1992); Terrance L. Tiessen, *Who Can Be Saved? Reassessing Salvation in Christ and World Religions* (IVP, 2004).

70. John Stott, *The Authentic Jesus* (Marshall, Morgan and Scott, 1985), 83. See also J. I. Packer, "Evangelicals and the Way of Salvation," in *Evangelical Affirmations*, ed. Kenneth S. Kantzer and Carl F. H. Henry (Zondervan, 1990), 121–23; Erickson, *How Shall They Be Saved?*; and David Clark, "Is Special Revelation Necessary for Salvation?" in *Through No Fault of Their Own?*, ed. William V. Crockett, and James Sigountos (Baker, 1991), 40–41.

71. Erickson, *How Shall They Be Saved?*, 158.

72. Lesslie Newbigin, *A Word in Season: Perspectives on Christian World Missions* (Eerdmans, 1994), 122, 115.

73. Johannes Verkuyl, "The Biblical Notion of Kingdom: Test of Validity for Theology of Religion," in *Good News of the Kingdom*, ed. Charles Van Engen, Dean S. Gillialand, and Paul Pierson (Orbis, 1993), 77.